The Story of Paul's Journey to Rome

Acts 27:1–44 for children

Written by Claire Miller • Illustrated by Unada Gleiwe

Arch® Books
Copyright © 2002 Concordia Publishing House
3558 S. Jefferson Avenue, St. Louis, MO 63118-3968
Manufactured in the United States of America

Printed in Colombia

Paul traveled 'round the world to preach
And tell of Jesus' love.
He said, "You're saved! Believe in Him—
You'll go to heaven above."

Paul's enemies were most upset.
"He's telling lies," they said.
"Arrest that man! Get rid of him!
We'd like to see him dead!"

So Paul was made a prisoner.
He was no longer free.
His trial would be far away—
In Rome, across the sea.

Paul and some other prisoners
Climbed on a great big ship.
Strong soldiers also went aboard
To guard them on the trip.

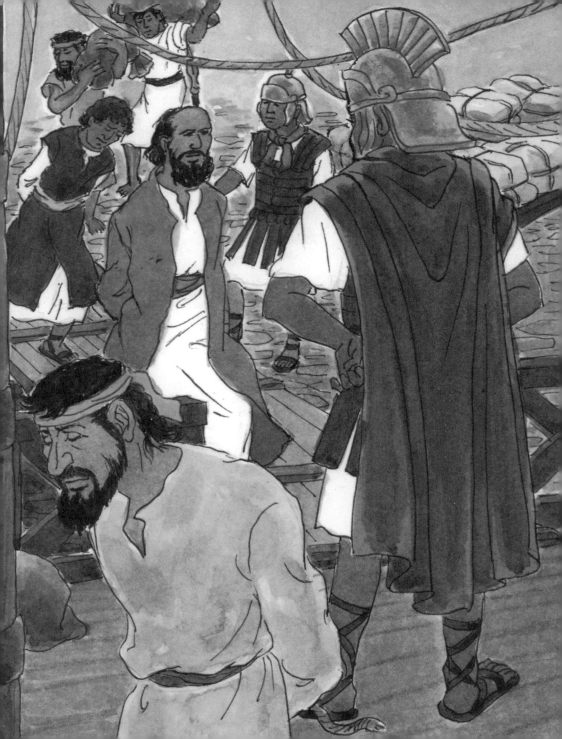

Paul warned the captain of the ship,
"It's dangerous to sail.
The winter storms are coming with
Strong winds, and rain, and hail.

"We really ought to wait till spring,
And sail the calmer seas.
If we go now, our ship will crash—
So listen to me, PLEASE!"

A gentle wind began to blow;
The captain couldn't wait.
The ship sailed off, but strong winds came.
By then it was too late.

The ship was blown far out to sea.
There was no turning back.
The rain poured down, the waves were rough;
For days the sky was black.

The people cried, "We won't survive!
Our ship is going down!"
But Paul said, "I've good news for you.
God promised we won't drown.

"God's angel said our ship will crash,
No matter what we try.
But God wants me to get to Rome,
And none of us will die."

For 14 days the storm roared on.
And then the sailors said,
"We're getting close to land, it seems.
If we hit rocks, we're dead!"

Paul said, "God promised we'd be safe,
Let's eat this food I found."
He took some bread, thanked God, and ate,
And passed it all around.

The folks were feeling stronger when
Ka-boom, ka-bash, BEWARE!
The ship got stuck in sand, and then
Some big waves wrecked it there.

The people hit the water fast,
And hurried to the beach.
As God had promised, all were safe.
Then Paul began to preach.

He told of Jesus' saving love
To everyone on shore.
And when he got to Rome, of course,
He praised God even more.

God keeps His promises to us,
Just as He did to Paul.
Believe in Jesus; you'll be saved:
Wow! That's the best of all!

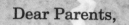

Dear Parents,

Paul had a burning desire to share the Good News of Jesus with new believers. He journeyed from city to city, always leaving behind small groups of believers who spread the Gospel to others. After being arrested for preaching the Gospel, he was sent to Rome for trial.

Paul was put aboard a large ship with 275 other passengers at a dangerous time of year. When the stormy weather hit, safe arrival seemed unlikely. But God promised Paul that no one would drown, even though the ship would be destroyed.

Explain to your child that just as God was with Paul and the others during their dangerous trip, He is also with us at all times. We can talk to God when we're afraid, and He will hear us. And just as God kept His promises to Paul, He keeps His promises to us. Best of all is the amazing promise of salvation through our faith in Jesus Christ.

The Author